WELCOME TO SKARA BRAE

The site you are visiting is extremely old. People were living here before the pyramids were built in Egypt. By the time Stonehenge was constructed in England, Skara Brae had already been abandoned, after about 300 to 400 years of continuous habitation.

Two things make this an extraordinary place. The first is its situation. At the time when it was occupied, Orkney was an enormously important place – perhaps one of the main power centres in Europe. In recognition of its significance, this part of the mainland has been designated a World Heritage Site.

Above: A carved-stone object, one of a number found at the site. Their purpose is unknown.

Opposite: Looking through the doorway into House 7.

The second is its remarkably good condition. Although their roofs are long gone, the stone walls and interior furnishings of several houses have survived almost intact. Skara Brae is the best-preserved Neolithic village in northern Europe and its remains allow us extraordinary insights into life as it was lived here 4,500 years ago.

CONTENTS

HIGHLIGHTS

◀ THE HOUSES
Nine of the dwellings survive, in varying states of completeness. Little remains of House 3, which has been swept away by the sea. Aside from House 7, all the other houses can be viewed from the walkway (p.8).

◀ THE REPLICA HOUSE
Before visiting the site be sure to explore this replica of a complete house. It is closely modelled on House 7, the best-preserved structure on the site, which has been sealed off for its protection and is not accessible to the public (p.12).

▲ THE EXHIBITION
It's well worth spending some time in the visitor centre before walking the short distance to the site. The displays carry a host of information about the Neolithic village and how its occupants may have lived (p.12).

◀ THE PREHISTORIC LANDSCAPE
Skara Brae is one of a group of extraordinary Neolithic monuments collectively recognised as a UNESCO World Heritage Site. It also includes other settlements, stone circles and burial cairns (p.52).

◄ THE WILDLIFE

Orkney's Atlantic coast provides a habitat for many seabirds, sea mammals, fish and shellfish, which helped provide a rich and varied diet for Skara Brae's residents. The ground is also fertile, allowing both arable farming and an abundance of wild flora (p.26).

▲ THE PASSAGES

The core of the last village on the site had become semi-subterranean, helping to shield the occupants from the elements. Access into and around the village was therefore via a network of passages, which still survive (p.19).

▲ THE WORKSHOP

The building known as Structure 8 clearly had a different function from the others. It is thought that it was used as a workshop, perhaps for making tools from flint and chert (p.20).

◄ SKAILL HOUSE

Originally built in the 1600s, Skaill House was the home of William Watt, the landowner who discovered Skara Brae in 1850. Now considered Orkney's finest mansion, it lies close to the site and is open to visitors from April to October (p.48).

SKARA BRAE AT A GLANCE

The site is reached by a path from the visitor centre which uses a trail of plaques to help demonstrate how old Skara Brae is.

On arriving at the cluster of houses, follow the path around it in a clockwise direction. Please stay on the path and do not step on any of the walls: they are very fragile.

The guided tour on the pages that follow begins with the replica house just beyond the visitor centre. It is not a house-by-house commentary, but refers to aspects of the site in the order in which you will find them.

Site staff will be happy to assist you in exploring the village and discovering its features.

1 HOUSE 1

One of the largest houses surviving in the village, and one of the best-preserved, though part of its north wall has been lost to the sea.

2 HOUSE 2

Significantly smaller than House 1, but its furniture is organised in much the same arrangement.

3 HOUSE 3

Almost all of this house has been lost to erosion so we cannot be sure how big it was, though we can assume its design was very similar to that of the other houses.

4 HOUSE 4

The easternmost house in the village, its layout mirrors that of House 1 and House 2.

5 HOUSE 5

Lying at the centre of the village, House 5 is well protected. Its storage cells are particularly well preserved.

6 HOUSE 6

The smallest house on the site, with few distinctive features.

7 HOUSE 7

The most complete house in the village, House 7 has been covered over for its protection. It cannot be accessed by visitors, but was used as the model for the replica house.

8 STRUCTURE 8

Separated from the other buildings, and equipped with different furniture, this is thought to have been a workshop of some kind.

9 HOUSE 9

One of the earliest houses visible on the site, its bed recesses are built into the walls rather than projecting into the living space.

10 HOUSE 10

Belonging to the same building phase as House 9, but less well preserved.

11 RANGERS' HUT

As well as an office for the Orkney Rangers, this small building holds a computer display allowing visitors to experience a 'virtual tour' inside the houses.

The photographs of objects included in this book are not shown to scale. Some of the objects can be seen in the visitor centre exhibition, while others are displayed at the Orkney Museum in Kirkwall and the National Museum of Scotland in Edinburgh.

AN OVERVIEW

Skara Brae is the best-preserved prehistoric
village in northern Europe. It's so important that
Indiana Jones was seen lecturing about the site
in one of his movies, *Indiana Jones and the Kingdom
of the Crystal Skull* (2008).

What makes this Neolithic settlement so special is that the
houses still contain the main items of furniture. Nowhere else
can you get such a clear idea of what the interior of houses
occupied by an early farming community some 4,500 years
ago actually looked like. Of course, you still have to use your
imagination to light the fire in the central hearth, to fill the
beds with bedding, to put objects on the dresser.

The individual houses, linked by passages, cluster together, forming
a tight-knit community. Most of what you see today is the remains
of the village at the end of its occupation, around 2600 or 2500 BC.
It comprises Houses 1 to 7 and a workshop, known as Structure 8.
At an earlier stage, the village had no passages, although the houses
were still close together. Some of the earlier houses are under those
of the later village but two, Houses 9 and 10, are not covered in
this way. The earlier village was occupied around 2900 BC.

Part of the village was washed away during a major storm in 1924
and it seems likely that other buildings were destroyed by earlier
storms. This means we cannot know how big the village was,
or easily estimate how many people lived there. Excavations at
other villages in Orkney suggest that we might expect there to
have been around 10 to 12 houses here at any one time. A village
of this size might have had 70 or more inhabitants. But nowhere
has a complete village been excavated, so it is possible that they
were much larger.

The narrow passages and the small doorways to the houses
might suggest that the people living at Skara Brae were rather small.
But this isn't the case. From skeletons found under the floor of
House 7 and others recovered from contemporary burial mounds
we know that they were pretty much the same size as us,
perhaps an inch or two shorter but that's all. The small size
of the passages and doors were all about staying warm by
keeping heat loss to a minimum.

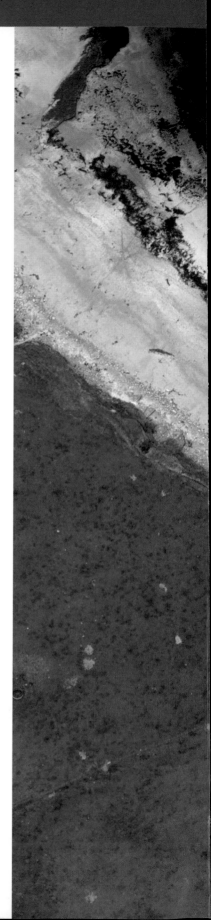

This page: An aerial photograph of the site. When it was first occupied, the shoreline was much further away, though it grew closer during the centuries when people lived here. We cannot be sure how much of the settlement has been lost to the sea.

THE HOUSES

The surviving buildings at Skara Brae are remarkably similar to each other. The main building material was stone, which would have been readily available from the coastal rock formations nearby.

As far as we can tell, all the houses were built in the same way. The outer and inner faces of the walls are dry stone, that is without mortar. The space between these two faces is filled with packed midden (see page 25). This created a very broad wall, often more than 2m thick. The midden core, together with clay beneath the wall and on its outer face, kept the houses wind- and waterproof.

We have very little evidence for the form and nature of the roofs. Some whalebone ribs have been found, suggesting they might have been used as rafters, but they have not occurred in sufficient numbers to be the principal material used. It has often been thought that the roofs would have been kept low to ameliorate the effects of high winds, but recent studies have proposed a high sloping roof thatched with eel grass.

In the centre of each house there is a large hearth. The fire would probably have been kept burning all the time. It provided both heat and light for those living in the house.

Above left: A view into House 1, the most complete house visitors can see on the site. Like all the others, it has a dresser opposite the doorway, a hearth at its centre and bed enclosures on both sides.

Left: House 5, a slightly smaller example than House 1, but with the same basic layout.

In order to keep the houses as warm as possible the doorway was kept very small – not much more than about 1m high and 50cm wide. At roughly the midpoint of each doorway there is an upright slab, projecting a few centimetres above the floor, and an equivalent slab projecting from the top of the doorway. Slabs of stone or wood could be set against these and held in place by a bar running in bar-holes set in the side walls. In other words, these doors could only be locked from the inside. They were not simply about protecting property but about privacy, allowing occupants to withdraw from the wider community.

The thick walls did more than keep the house warm and dry. They made possible the creation of cells within the wall. Most were quite small and seem to have been for storage. But, principally on the evidence of House 7, there seems to have been one cell in each house that was much higher. This cell appears to have been connected to drains that run under the houses. In that case it is likely to have been an indoor toilet, the earliest we know of in Britain.

Above: A doorway, seen from the inside.

Above: An illustration of the same doorway, showing how it would look when the door was held in place by a bar.

THE FURNITURE

What makes Skara Brae so special is the presence of furniture in the houses. Because it was made of stone, the furniture has survived, allowing us to see how the residents organised their living spaces.

Two features of the Orkney environment have combined to give us this remarkable glimpse of prehistoric life. First, the wind and, to a lesser extent, the salt spray from the sea have meant that very few trees grow on Orkney. When they do, in sheltered spots, they are still rather small. And second, the local flagstone can be easily split into slabs that resemble wooden planks. Indeed, all of the main pieces look like stone versions of wooden furniture.

We see this most clearly in the box beds projecting from the walls of the later houses. These are, of course, just the skeletons of the beds and you have to imagine them filled with fleeces and plants like bracken to make them comfortable. At the front corners of the beds there were upright columns and these seem to have supported canopies that would have been tied back to the wall. Perhaps these were like four-poster beds, with curtains made of skins to help keep out draughts.

The dresser on the wall opposite the door also shows aspects of early woodworking with shelves made of stone 'planks' supported by angular stone uprights that would have been round if made from wood. More recently, dressers have often been used to enhance status through the display of valuable items. That may have been the purpose of these dressers as they dominate the view of anyone entering the low, narrow doorway. But they may equally have been the equivalent of an altar or shrine, or multi-purpose, like a grand mantelpiece.

Above: One of the bed enclosures in House 7.

Above: The dresser in House 7.

Set into the floor of all the later houses are a number of stone boxes. Each has a flat slab forming the base with four slabs forming the sides. There is no evidence that they had lids. The gaps between the slabs were sealed with clay – rather like the way putty is used in a modern window to seal the joint between the glass and the window frame. This meant that they were watertight.

These boxes may have been used to soak limpets for use as fish bait. Since this takes 24 to 48 hours, the household would have required several boxes to ensure a ready supply of fresh bait. Large numbers of limpet shells were found during the excavation, yet within living memory limpets have only ever been eaten as starvation food. They make excellent fish bait if they have been soaked. With no evidence of a lack of food at Skara Brae, it therefore seems likely that they were collected for bait.

In every house, upright slabs were used to divide off an area. Usually, this was from the side of one of the beds to the wall close to the doorway. This area would have provided a secure storage area, perhaps for materials stored in some of the large pots found at the site. Fragments recovered during excavation come from pots with rim diameters as great as 60cm. Pots of this size would have been extremely heavy to move about. Instead, they would have been kept in the same place and the upright slab would have protected them from breakage by kicking or knocking.

Below: Two watertight stone boxes on the floor of House 5.
It is thought they were used to soak limpets for fish bait.

BEFORE YOU VISIT THE SITE

There are two things to do before you go to the site itself. These will help you understand the site better and get the most out of your visit.

First, you should visit the exhibition in the visitor centre. It displays some of the objects that have been found at the site and explores many aspects of life at Skara Brae and beyond. Second, you should visit the replica house immediately outside the visitor centre.

The replica house is based on House 7, the best-preserved of the village's houses. For reasons discussed on pages 16–17, House 7 cannot be viewed at the site. The replica house, though, provides a very good idea of what it was like. It also enables you to gain an impression of life in one of these houses. This is not possible at the site itself because visitors cannot go inside the houses.

Below: Inside the replica house, closely modelled on House 7.

Below: The roof of the replica house. Its structure is based on careful research, though modern materials have been used.

Right: A square stone vessel on display in the visitor centre. It was used for preparing ochre pigments for use as dye or paint.

Below: A sandstone tool with teeth, on display in the visitor centre. It may have been a hand-held rake, though we cannot be sure how it was used.

Although it is based on House 7, the replica house is like every house in the later village. This is because each house is organised in the same way. The dresser is on the wall opposite the door, with the hearth at the centre of the floor. The box beds project from the walls to right and left with storage recesses placed above them.

Nowhere else in northern Europe can give us a comparable understanding of what a prehistoric dwelling looked like, but when looking at the real houses it is important to remember the things that are missing. There is nothing, like skins and fleeces or bracken, to soften the harshness of the stone. Nor is it easy for us to get a sense of living with only the light given off by the fire – and perhaps simple lamps burning animal oil, though none have been found. What is almost certainly missing is the use of coloured pigments to decorate the house.

So, although the replica house helps a great deal to imagine what the houses were like to live in, you have to use your imagination to enhance the pictures.

Above right: A basin made from the hollowed-out vertebra of a whale and now displayed in the visitor centre.

This page: House 9, the best-preserved house from the earlier period of house-building at Skara Brae. Its bed enclosures are recessed into the side walls, unlike those in the later houses.

THE EARLY VILLAGE

We know that there was an earlier village at Skara Brae. Although it was not the earliest occupation of the site, it lies largely under the later one. Only two of its houses were not covered by the later village.

The best-preserved houses of the early village are Houses 9 and 10. They lie on the south side of the site, farthest away from the sea. Excavation has shown that this early village stretched across most of the area of the later village. Although set close together, the houses of the early village were not semi-subterranean but freestanding, with paths between them.

The houses in the early village had the same basic layout as the later houses. There was a central hearth and a dresser opposite the door. But the beds did not project from the side walls, as they do in the later houses. Instead each bed is set into the thickness of the wall to form a bed recess. These can be seen best in House 9, where the dresser is nearest to you and the door farthest away. As in the later houses, the beds are on the right and left sides of the house.

Houses 9 and 10 appear quite small compared to the houses of the later village but this was not true of all the houses in the early village. Excavation between the main passage and House 7 discovered part of a house that was as big as any of the later houses.

Above: House 10, the less well-preserved of the two early houses that can now be seen. Other houses from this earlier period are concealed beneath the later village.

Below: A cross-section of part of the site shows how remains of earlier structures are buried beneath layers of sand, with later structures built over them. The blue represents midden; the green is the old land surface.

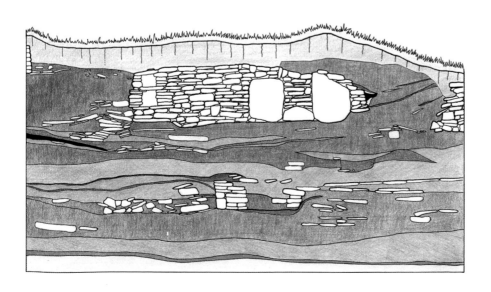

HOUSE 7

House 7 was the only one in the later village that had not been investigated to some degree before the main archaeological work at the site in the 1920s. It is the best-preserved house, but you can't see it at the moment, for reasons linked to those excavations and what happened next.

Because this house was so well preserved, with all the walls standing more than 3 metres high, the Office of Works (forerunner of Historic Scotland) wanted to display it while at the same time protecting it. Some of the other houses had been left open to the weather and it is possible that significant features were lost. So they put a concrete collar on top of the walls to support a glass roof with sliding panels. These panels were opened during visiting hours and closed at night.

Unfortunately, the long-term effect was the opposite of what was intended. The glass roof did not protect the house, but damaged it – in two ways. First, the weight of the concrete collar and the glass roof compressed the walls. And second, the glass acted like a greenhouse, warming up the house during the day and cooling it at night. The range of temperature and humidity that resulted started to crack and break the stones in the wall.

To stop this damage getting worse, Historic Scotland has removed the glass, replaced it with a lightweight turf roof and sealed the doorway. Conservators have taken laser scans of the walls and established fixed points that will enable them to measure any change in the condition of the walls. The environment in the house is constantly measured. It shows that the temperature and humidity are now stabilised. These are the first essential steps to ensure its long-term future.

Top left: The interior of House 7, no longer accessible to the public.

Centre left: Dismantling the glass roof in 2007.

Bottom left: Laser-scanning the interior of House 7 in 2010. The three-dimensional laser scan will form a permanent record of the house.

CONSERVING SKARA BRAE

Everything that you see on the site has to be conserved and looked after in order to keep it in good condition. The need for preservation affects the way you visit the site – where you can go and where you can't.

Conservation of ancient monuments such as Skara Brae is essential if future generations are to enjoy coming to the site as much as we do today. Historic Scotland has to have this long-term view. This is why House 7 is currently closed.

The biggest threat comes from the sea as it continually erodes the soft coastline of the Bay of Skaill. It washed away most of House 3 when the site first came into the care of the State. The whole of 1925 and 1926 saw the building of an initial sea wall to protect the site before any archaeological work could be undertaken. That wall has had to be extended and strengthened on several occasions since.

Protecting the site is not just about keeping the sea out. The sea is most threatening at the time of storms, when wind also becomes an important factor, blowing sand into the houses and passages. Left unprotected, the structures would soon fill with sand, on which plants would eventually establish themselves. Some plants would even grow between the stones of the walls. Dealing with all of this is an ongoing process.

Equally important to the wellbeing of the site is the way visitors experience it. The doors of the houses and the passages are very narrow, with low headroom. If visitors were allowed access to these areas there would inevitably be accidental damage or alteration to the structures, aside from the crowding that would result.

Although the stones give the impression of strength and solidity, many of them are in fact quite fragile. Regular handling would impart a polish to some and destroy others. Neither is desirable. This is why visitors look down into the houses rather than go in them.

Above: Visitors at Skara Brae in 1955. Without restricting visitor access, the site cannot be properly protected and damage is inevitable.

THE CARVINGS

A large number of decorated stones have been found at Skara Brae. They range from apparent doodles to elaborate patterns. Some are still built into the walls.

Some of the site's more exposed carvings are protected by glass plates – for example in the open cell to the west of House 7. The same geometric designs are found on a small number of the bone and stone tools, and on many of the fragments of pot found at the site.

The known decoration is concentrated in those areas of the site that were previously undisturbed – in House 7 and Structure 8, and in the passages. This suggests that decoration was once more widespread but exposure of some areas to the weather has led to its erosion.

Finely incised lines form most of the designs. These were made with a sharp-pointed implement, probably made of flint. A few have pecked decoration. Many are lightly scratched with little sense of organisation in their patterns. It has been suggested that these formed the base for painted decoration. Pots of stone, bone and shell at the site have all been employed to mix colouring material using red ochre.

The most organised designs use lozenges and triangles as their key elements. Some have been interpreted as landscape drawings showing the view to Hoy or perhaps mainland Scotland. But lozenges and triangles occur naturally on outcrops of flagstone. Perhaps their adoption in the Skara Brae decorations was intended to emphasise an affinity with the landscape.

Below: A three-dimensional laser scan of a lozenge-shaped carving found on the exterior wall of Structure 8.

Below: Similar motifs found carved on one of the box-bed slabs in House 7.

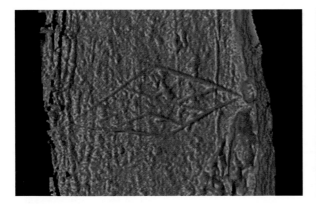

THE PASSAGES

The covered passages are one of the unique features of Skara Brae. They have not been found at any of the comparable sites on Orkney.

The main passage runs through the centre of the site, roughly south-west to north-east. Originally, it was roofed throughout its length. It seems that the creation of the passages took place late in the occupation of the second village when the houses were rendered semi-subterranean. Excavations between the main passage and House 7 showed that the area here must have been open until almost the end of the settlement's life.

Passages would not have been necessary if the houses were not semi-subterranean. The decision to build them may well have coincided with attempts to separate the houses from the rest of the village. The walls between House 2 and Structure 8 and beyond the entrance to the main passage to the south-east are revetment walls, designed to contain the mounds of occupation material surrounding the houses.

The western entrance to the main passage has a doorway similar to those of the houses. Like those doors, it is about privacy and exclusion, not necessarily security. It is not clear why an increased level of separation of the houses from the rest of the village was thought necessary near the end of life in the village.

Above: Inside the main passage that gave access to the houses.

STRUCTURE 8 - THE WORKSHOP

At the western edge of the village is a different kind of building. We cannot be certain how it was used, but the evidence suggests it was industrial rather than domestic.

Structure 8 has a rather pear-shaped interior, with recesses and working areas. It has no beds, no dresser and no boxes, so it cannot have been a house. It was never surrounded by midden and was instead always a freestanding structure. It was a workshop.

When this workshop was excavated in 1929 by Gordon Childe, he found the floor covered with hundreds of fragments of dark chert, a locally available rock from which small tools could be made.

Above: The paved area outside Structure 8, sometimes known as the 'market place'.

Top: Inside Structure 8. Although superficially similar to the other structures, it includes no beds and was almost certainly used as a workshop.

This chert seems to have been used instead of flint in the latest phase of occupation of the village. Flint is a glass-like rock that can be chipped and flaked into shape to create tools with a sharp cutting edge. It forms as nodules within chalk and would only have been available in Orkney as beach pebbles eroding from chalk beds under the sea.

Chert was a poor but necessary substitute. It is more difficult to work than flint, and seems only to have been used when the supply of flint was interrupted, or dwindled away.

Chert can be made easier to use through a process known as heat pre-treatment. In this process, chunks of chert are completely covered by pieces of igneous rock that have been heated to as high a temperature as possible. The igneous rock takes a long time to cool. After being heated and slowly cooled in this way, chert is much easier to make into tools.

There are suggestions that this process took place in Structure 8. At the sea-facing end of the building, there is a narrow break in the wall. It's too narrow to be an entrance. As it faces into the prevailing wind it may be a flue that helped raise the temperature of a fire when the igneous rock was being heated up. Lumps of heated igneous rock were found on either side of this opening, inside the building.

Stone tools would normally be produced in the open air. The process doesn't take very long, but sharp flakes can fly off at some speed, and at unpredictable angles. It's best to have a clear area around you.

Large and imposing workshops for making stone tools have not been identified anywhere else in Scotland. So, perhaps, Structure 8 was intended not just for the production of small stone tools. This workshop may be where many of the objects found on the site were made. After all, many of the large carved-stone objects and the various pieces of bone jewellery would have taken longer to make.

Top right: A small axe-head of polished brown flint found at the site.

Right: A pendant found on the site, made from decorated and polished bone. Jewellery like this may have been made in the workshop.

IDENTICAL LAYOUTS

As we mentioned in discussing the replica house, all the houses at Skara Brae have the same basic layout. Each had a central hearth, a dresser opposite the entrance and box beds to left and right.

The easiest place on the site to see this is at Houses 1 and 2. As you stand looking into them you are above the wall that contains the doorways. Against the far wall is the large dresser with the central hearth in front of it. Projecting from the walls to the right and left are the stone enclosures that formed the box beds.

Below: House 1, with dresser, hearth, bed enclosures and limpet boxes clearly visible.

This layout is used in all the houses. It must have made all of them appear very similar but that doesn't mean that they were indistinguishable from one another. Small variations were possible, for instance, in the number of the clay-luted stone boxes or the position of marked-off storage areas. These similarities in layout, together with the way the houses cluster tightly together, suggests a community with high levels of conformity and strongly established ways of behaviour.

Perhaps, though, because we can only see the skeletons of the furniture, we over-emphasise the levels of conformity. As you bent double to enter the house through the small and narrow doorway, the dresser would have dominated your view, its contents lit by the flickering fire. Changing displays on each dresser, for example, might well have made every house seem very different to the people who lived at Skara Brae.

Below: House 7, with its furniture arranged in a similar way.

THE CELLS

Each of the houses at Skara Brae has cells let into the thickness of the walls. These were almost certainly used for storage, though there is very little evidence to tell us what was stored.

House 5 is a good place to see the form of these storage cells. It does not stand to the same height as some of the other houses, so we can see the cells let into the thickness of the walls. On the far side of the house, a cell can be seen that would have been hidden behind the dresser. There is a second cell to the left of this one.

We have very little evidence to enable us to understand what these cells were used for. Most were already empty when the site was excavated. But in 1927 a cell in the west wall of House 1 was found to contain more than 3,250 bone beads, as well as other bone jewellery and tools. This may be exceptional, but it suggests that the cells were used as places to keep valuable objects – and perhaps the raw materials to make those objects.

Several houses have cells like House 5 that could only have been accessed by crawling under the dresser. These inaccessible cells conjure up ideas about security but also perhaps special places associated with beliefs.

Cell	
Bed	
Hearth	
Dresser	
Entrance	
Limpet box	
Storage area	

Passage

Top left: One of the storage cells is clearly visible in House 5.

Above: A plan of House 1 shows how the space was divided up. A vast cache of jewellery and tools was found in the large cell in the west (left) wall.

Right: A pendant found at the site. Made by boring a hole through an animal's canine tooth, it is almost 7.5cm long.

Far right: Bone jewellery found at the site. We cannot be sure how individual beads and pendants were strung – this necklace and bracelet were strung for display purposes.

EROSION

Even before the site was discovered, some of its buildings had been washed away by coastal erosion. This has been, and remains, an ongoing problem.

The danger that the sea poses to the site has already been discussed (page 17). Adjacent to House 1 are the remnants of House 3. The rest was washed away during a major storm in December 1924, soon after the Office of Works had taken the site into care. It was this damage that prompted the construction of the sea wall.

In front of the doorway of House 3, the only recognisable part to survive, is a hatch covering part of one of the drains that run across the site under the floors of the houses.

MIDDEN

Midden is composed of the rubbish thrown away by the inhabitants of Skara Brae. Some things, like stone, bone or shell, survive largely in the condition they were in when they were deposited. But a larger part of the midden was composed of material like plants and remnants of flesh attached to the bones that in time will rot down in the same way as the compost heap in your garden. The final important component was ash from the hearths.

Once midden had rotted down to something not very different from garden soil it was mixed with clay and sand to be used as a building material. Large quantities of midden were packed between the inner and outer faces of the house walls. Towards the end of the later village, its build-up helped render the houses semi-subterranean.

Left: An example of midden, found at Jarlshof in Shetland. Rich in seashells, it reveals something of the occupants' diet.

Top left: The remnants of House 3, almost all of which has been lost to the sea.

Top right: Orkney's west coast is frequently buffeted by storms.

THE WILDLIFE OF SKAILL BAY

The Bay of Skaill lies on Orkney's Atlantic coast, facing the prevailing wind. This is a hostile environment, in which wildlife initially seems scarce. But closer examination will reveal a richer picture.

Sometimes the most obvious presence at Skara Brae is an inquisitive common or grey seal – both species are abundant along Orkney's coastlines.

Cockles, razor shells (or spoots) and other invertebrates can also be found on the beaches, burrowing into the sand as the tide goes out. Shore-feeding birds such as redshank, oystercatcher and curlew patrol the shoreline as the water level recedes, probing the sand with their bills. They have bills of different lengths, allowing each species to feed at a different depth, avoiding direct competition.

Between the sand and the land, the rocky foreshore is composed of exposed bedrock. These rocks contain fossils of some of the earliest known plants. Today, the bedrock is a habitat for plants that can withstand difficult conditions. Thrift, a pink-flowered plant that grows on sand, pebbles and rock near the sea shore, is well adapted to life on the edge. Constantly battered by salt-laden wind, it has developed tap roots that can go down many feet in search of fresh water. It also has thin, grass-like leaves to reduce moisture loss, and its dense tufts retain water like a sponge.

Beyond the shoreline there are coastal grasslands. Where they have been left unfarmed, they harbour a community of flowering plants adapted to life near the shore, such as tufted vetch and bird's foot trefoil. Both of these plants are members of the pea family, which have nodules on their roots. Bacteria living in these nodules perform the very useful task of taking nitrogen from the air and converting it into fertiliser.

Bird's foot trefoil, with its tiny, clover-like yellow flowers, is found all over Orkney. Many people know this flower as 'bacon and eggs' – the nickname refers to the vibrant red and yellowy-orange colour of the flowers when they begin to open.

Top: Common seal, an abundant species around Orkney's coastlines.

Above: Lapwing, often seen near farmland and identifiable by its unusual flight pattern.

Some flowers can pollinate themselves if necessary, but they are usually cross-pollinated by bees and other insects. The rare great yellow bumble bee and the moss carder bee can often be seen feeding on these plants. Both species are only found in the north of Scotland. The moss carder has a striking bright orange upper body and yellowish lower body.

Above left: Thrift and bird's foot trefoil growing near the site.

Above right: A great yellow bumble bee.

The wetland just north of the site contains specialised plants including the striking yellow flag iris. Roots of yellow flag iris were discovered during the excavation of the site. It is possible that they were eaten; however, they have an unpleasant acrid taste. We can only speculate how the iris might have been used, but historically it has provided a source of black dyes. There is also evidence dating back almost 2,000 years for its use as a medicine – an emetic, a purgative and a cure for diarrhoea. In medieval times it was used to stop bleeding.

Birds associated with grassland and wetland can be at least heard if not seen. Reed bunting is typically found in wet vegetation. The male is often seen perched on top of a reed and singing. Lapwing (also known as the peewit in imitation of its display call) can often be spotted in the surrounding farmland with its distinctive wavering flight.

Skylark thrives on the short grass found in the area. With its distinctive loud, warbling call, it can be spotted, often with some difficulty, as a small dot at great height when it is doing its distinctive song flight. The skylark's brown plumage makes it hard to see on the ground. Numbers of all these birds have declined significantly in recent years and there are now concerns for their future conservation.

LIFE AT SKARA BRAE

This page: An artist's impression shows residents herding cattle near the village.

Skara Brae was abandoned about 4,500 years ago, yet a remarkable amount of evidence survives. From careful examination of this, and a knowledge of other Neolithic sites, we can draw some conclusions about how people lived here.

Everything in the archaeological evidence suggests that the people living at Skara Brae were well fed, mainly through rearing cattle, sheep and pigs. Fully able to meet the needs of their lives, they clearly knew the local environment extremely well and exploited much that it had to offer. Other rarer materials, such as haematite from Hoy, were probably acquired through contacts with other settlements.

THE SETTING

Nowadays Skara Brae is situated on the Bay of Skaill, with the highest tides kept out only by a protective wall. Yet when the site was first occupied, the sea lay away to the west.

The underlying flagstone falls gently away to the north and east from a high point in the south-west. On top of the flagstone is an old land surface; a clayey layer incorporating fragments of weathered bedrock. Above this, across the site, is a deep layer of sterile sand. This natural build-up of sand has usually been seen as a windblown accumulation against the underlying slope of the bedrock.

More recently, it has been suggested that the sand was a water-borne deposit resulting from a tsunami event. Whatever its origins, the sand helped to level out the surface to a very gentle slope. It seems possible that grass established itself on this sand surface, providing a greensward running down to the small lochans that filled the area of the present bay.

This provided a very suitable site for settlement by an early farming community. The earliest occupation has a wide date-range but the best estimates are that it took place in the two centuries between 3360 and 3160 BC. The deposits associated with this occupation were only certainly recognised in the 1972–3 excavations, and are therefore very limited in extent. No structures can be associated with them, but they give the clear impression that they derive from cleaning floors and hearths. This suggests that buildings were close by.

Following this occupation, the site seems to have been abandoned for two or more centuries before settlement resumed on the site. This lengthy break combines with a number of special features to suggest that these were the first settlers in this area. Once work began around 2900 BC on the earlier of the two villages we can see on the site today, settlement seems to have been continuous for 300 or 400 years. In this long timespan, many modifications to individual structures took place. Some structures were completely abandoned. There was certainly another major sand blow during this occupation.

It is clear that, from the first occupation until the end of the later village, the inhabitants exploited a wide range of environments in the area around the settlement. Exploiting both fresh- and seawater environments, they obtained foodstuffs from the surrounding land as well as from lochs, streams and offshore waters.

Pollen analysis suggests a locally treeless and largely pastoral landscape, not very different from that of today. But the latest excavations recovered evidence of 17 different types of native Scottish trees and shrubs. There is some suggestion that areas of mixed oak woodland might have been still in existence a few miles away.

This page: The Bay of Skaill
seen from the air, with the
Loch of Harray beyond.

WHAT KIND OF SETTLEMENT WAS SKARA BRAE?

Ever since the archaeological investigation of the site in the 1920s it has been usual to regard the village at Skara Brae as the home of a farming community. The people who lived here did not grow crops but they kept cows, sheep and pigs and these were their principal sources of food, supplemented by some hunting and fishing. That interpretation provides the framework and underpins the statements in this book.

But the evidence is far from conclusive. Villages like Skara Brae are almost unknown among the early farming communities in Britain, where the individual farmstead was the norm. Why, then, should farmers in Orkney decide to live in villages, and more especially in communities that appear to have required high levels of conformity? There is no immediate or obvious answer.

In these circumstances, it seems reasonable to consider other possibilities. There are several that have reasonable fits with the available evidence but, like the idea that it was a straightforward community of farmers, none are without their problems.

Above: The interior of one of the houses as it may have looked when occupied.

To our eyes, the remarkable conformity in the shape of the houses and the layout of their furniture suggests a religious rather than a secular community. Was it then the home of religious leaders? The decorated stones and the remarkable carved-stone objects occur in much larger numbers than in other excavated villages and find comparison only among the structures being excavated at the Ness of Brodgar in the religious centre of Mainland. In this case, the material found in the middens could be considered offerings from the wider community.

Equally, though, the village could be considered the home of a secular elite. In this case the conformity might well be a device to ensure that the solidarity of this ruling group was not threatened by individual aspirations. The decorated stones and the carved-stone objects would in this case be symbols of secular power. In these circumstances the middens' contents would represent tribute.

Other material from the site suggests yet another interpretation: that this was the home of craft workers. The sheer quantity of beads and clear evidence of their manufacture might be one such pointer. There is also the presence of valuable raw materials, like the walrus tusks recovered in the excavations, from which pins and pendants would be manufactured. In this situation the material from the middens would be the product of exchange and barter.

This is, of course, to put the issues in terms of exclusive options. It is just as likely that the best explanation is a combination of these possibilities. Religious leaders might also be the secular elite, for instance. The point is really that the wealth of information from Skara Brae challenges the straightforward interpretations we might wish to adopt.

Right, centre and top: Two of the mysterious carved-stone objects found on the site.

Bottom right: A walrus tusk found on the site. It may have been intended for carving, or for use as a tool.

This page: The hearth of House 7. This may have been the only source of light within the houses.

HEATING, LIGHTING AND VENTILATION

Although the houses are relatively large, the conditions inside them would probably have seemed uncomfortable to us. They would have been warm but dark – and perhaps a little smoky too.

Fuel is one of the necessities of life. Without it you can't cook or, just as important in northern climes, stay warm. In the centre of each house and in Structure 8 there is a large hearth. The fire that burned here was probably kept permanently alight.

Keeping it burning involved collecting a range of fuels. The peat bogs that are now such a prominent feature in the Orkney landscape – and which in the more recent past have provided so much fuel – had not formed when Skara Brae was occupied. A surprising amount of timber may have arrived as driftwood from North America, but it seems to have been too precious to burn as fuel. Turf, seaweed, animal dung and the bones of whales and seals, rich in oil, were the main sources of fuel.

The hearth didn't just heat the house and provide a place to cook, it was also the principal source of lighting. Although thousands of objects were found at Skara Brae, none of them can be definitely interpreted as a lamp, although small thumbpots and hollowed stones could have held oils. Firelight would seem a very poor light source for us, but the human eye can adapt to very low light levels. Even so, the houses would undoubtedly appear very dark to us.

There may have been a ventilation hole at the centre of the roof, allowing a small amount of daylight to enter, but it's unlikely. A hole to vent the smoke would have made it difficult to keep a fire burning during heavy rain, and would have allowed unwelcome heat loss. In these houses, smoke wasn't necessarily something you wanted to get rid of quickly. It enabled the occupants to preserve meat and fish hung amid the rafters. And just as important, over time, it would have helped to 'cure' the roofing materials, making them more waterproof.

Above: Animal bones found on the site. Wood was quite scarce, and it is possible that some bones were used as fuel.

FOOD

The principal source of food, then as now, was farming. This was supplemented by a wide range of other foodstuffs obtained in the area around the site.

The earliest inhabitants of the site grew barley, but we have no evidence that this continued during the life of either village. Instead the main foodstuffs seem to have come from the domesticated animals – cattle, sheep and pigs. These provided, among other cuts, beefsteak, veal, lamb and pork chops. And, of course, these animals would have yielded more than meat. Dairy products, particularly milk and cheese, might also have been important.

It is less clear where these animals were kept. The evidence of the more recent past in Orkney suggests that cattle in particular need to be brought in during the winter months. But byres have not been identified, either at Skara Brae or at any of the similar villages that have been excavated.

Equally important, at least in terms of a varied diet, was the residents' exploitation of what the surrounding areas had to offer. Wild plants were probably among the most important elements, but evidence for them rarely survives. At Skara Brae we have found only hazelnuts and crab apples.

Other gathered items are more identifiable. Chief among these is eggs. The finds from Skara Brae include shells from the eggs of 22 species. Although seabirds predominate because of their high density, nesting in large colonies, ducks and even some grassland species such as plover (now a gourmet food) were also taken when available. Shellfish such as mussels, cockles, whelks and crabs were also regularly collected – although the limpets gathered were most likely used as fish bait.

Left, top to bottom: The people who lived at Skara Brae farmed cattle and other livestock, hunted deer and obtained some of their food from the sea.

Right: Hazelnuts are one of the few wild plant foods that we can be sure were consumed at the site.

Hunting and fishing were also used to expand the range of foods, although that may well not have been the sole purpose of such activities. Red deer would certainly have provided a welcome taste of venison, but their antler was equally important. Some 46 species of bird are represented among the bird bones from the site, but again, feathers may have been as important a reason as food for their collection. Seabirds and wildfowl are the most important groups.

Fishing was similarly an occasional activity. Both sea fish, like cod, and freshwater species like eel and trout were caught. What is surprising is that apart from two possible fish spearheads there is no demonstrable fishing equipment among the objects from Skara Brae. There is similarly no surviving equipment that might point to the hunting of sea mammals, although even stranded animals would bring an abundance of food and other raw materials.

Above: Seabirds were certainly important to the villagers, probably for eggs and meat, but also perhaps for their feathers.

MEDICINE

Many plants were probably collected for their medicinal use, though they don't normally survive in the archaeological record. But among the more remarkable finds during the 1972–3 excavations were the outer skins of a number of puffballs — so many, in fact, that they must have been deliberately collected. What was missing was the cottony inner tissue. This material has been used in the recent past to help staunch bleeding and promote blood-clotting. It seems likely that these examples were collected for the same purpose. Rhizomes of the yellow flag iris were also found. These too have long been used as a herbal remedy, most usually as an emetic.

Right: Puffball fungi were collected by the villagers, perhaps for their medicinal properties.

CRAFT-WORKING

To judge by the materials from which they are made, it seems likely that most of the objects found at Skara Brae were made on the site.

As we have seen, Structure 8 is best interpreted as a workshop. It is possible that there were similar structures in the adjacent area which have since been lost to the sea. But some crafts, like bead-making, did not need a special place.

We know that flint and chert were fashioned into tools with a sharp cutting edge (see page 20). But in Orkney, flint only occurs as beach pebbles and the chert is found in small lumps. This means that only very small tools could be made from them. Also, making flint or chert tools is quite dangerous, because of the razor-sharp fragments that fly off in the process.

Top: Making Grooved Ware pots. Craft-working would have taken place outdoors when weather permitted, as the houses would have been dark.

Right: A Skaill knife – a simple cutting tool made by splitting a pebble. Many examples were found at the site and they would have been used for numerous purposes. This one is decorated with incised motifs similar to those found on the buildings.

Some larger tools were made from the local flagstone. These include 'Skaill knives' – simple cutting tools made by throwing a large pebble against another to produce an oval flake with a sharp edge and a thickened back. They were probably all-purpose tools with uses including the initial butchery of animals. But much of the tool-kit used for finer work on skins and other organic materials was fashioned from bone and wood.

Large amounts of debris from the manufacture of bone beads show that they were made at the site. Many of these beads are made from bone or the roots of cattle teeth. In both cases the cavity at the centre of the bone or tooth root provides a natural perforation. Manufacture of the larger pins is also suggested by the discovery of several unworked walrus tusks during the 19th-century excavations.

Many of the remarkable carved-stone objects are made from very hard volcanic rocks. These occur as dykes breaking through the flagstone at several points across the island. Working it into complex but balanced shapes without the use of metal must have taken considerable diligence and skill.

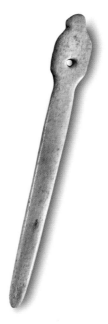

Above: A pin made from whalebone found at the site. About 16cm long, it was probably used to hold hair or clothing in place.

LEISURE PURSUITS

It seems unlikely that the people living at Skara Brae saw their time as divided into work and leisure as we do now. Many of their activities, such as hunting or fishing, may well have been both work and pleasure.

But there are a few objects that seem best interpreted as gaming pieces. The most important of these are two dice-like objects. These are not marked like modern dice. Instead a single face on each of them has five and two dots respectively. Two other sides on each of them have deep grooves, and the remaining faces are plain. It is not at all clear how these would have been used, or whether they were part of a larger set of gaming pieces. They are as likely to be used in telling the future as in gambling.

Right: Two dice-like objects found at the site and displayed in the visitor centre. It seems likely that they were used in some kind of game or divining activity.

CLOTHING AND JEWELLERY

There is no direct evidence for what kind of clothes people wore. On the other hand, we have large quantities of jewellery from Skara Brae, mainly consisting of pins, beads and pendants.

It does not appear that people at Skara Brae wore clothes made of fabric. None of the tools needed to make textiles were found, and the sheep at that time would not have produced much wool. Simple felting may have been carried out, but it would have required little equipment, and no evidence survives. All of this suggests that clothing was made from cured animal skins, perhaps even leather. Evidence was found for a large number of slaughtered calves – these would have provided very supple and soft skins. Just how fashioned the garments were is unclear.

It is usual to envisage pins as fastening clothing together. Some of the pins are certainly of the right size for this, but others are so large that they could not have been used in this way. These large and often elaborate pins were probably only worn on special occasions. Almost all of the surviving pins are made of bone, usually that of marine mammals, but a single rare find of the head of a large wooden pin in the 1972–3 excavations reminds us of another material that would have been used.

It is not clear whether the beads were strung as necklaces and bracelets, or sewn to clothing. Perhaps they were used for both, as beads were found in a variety of sizes and shapes – some tubes; some sequin-like. Although several thousand beads seems a large number, it is important to realise how many are needed to create a spectacular show. The regalia of the chiefs of the native North American Plains peoples often used more than 1,500 beads. Many of the pendants, particularly those made of marine mammal teeth, seem to have been worn together with the beads, but a small number were probably worn as individual items.

Above: Two villagers, shown here removing eels from eel-traps, wear simple tailored leather clothing and jewellery made from bone and teeth.

Centre right: A pendant found on the site, made from decorated and polished bone.

Above right: Some of the many bone beads found at the site. They have been strung as a necklace and a bracelet, though we cannot be sure exactly how they were originally used.

SOCIETY AND BELIEFS

Where written records survive, we normally know how a society was organised and what people believed. But when dealing with prehistoric communities, we do not have any texts. This means that anything we say about society or belief is very speculative.

What is clear at Skara Brae is that the houses are all pretty similar in size. If the community had a leader he did not, as we might expect, live in a larger house. It seems more likely that there was a shared leadership, with individuals taking the lead in activities they were known to be good at. One individual, for example, might have been in charge on fishing trips, while another led the community in animal husbandry. But the system cannot have been without disputes, and in such a close-knit community they must have had effective ways of dealing with them.

It is particularly difficult to find ways to access what people believed. Perhaps the strange carved-stone objects were used in religious rituals, but they might equally have been symbols of authority, used perhaps as much outside as inside the community.

The pieces of furniture we call dressers could have acted as shrines or altars. We simply don't know. And we can suggest that people from Skara Brae may have been involved with the ritual landscapes at Brodgar and Stenness, but we have no real understanding of the belief systems that lay behind their creation and use.

Right: Three of the carved-stone objects found at the site. Their significance remains unknown.

CONTACT WITH OTHER SETTLEMENTS

Today, it is easy to imagine Skara Brae as an isolated community, but it was not. We know that Neolithic Orkney was an important power centre with many links via sea routes.

Contact can be seen as operating at three levels. First, there is the contact with other settlements within Orkney that all inhabitants of Skara Brae might, and probably would, have experienced from time to time. Second, there would have been contact with other groups in Britain and Ireland: this may well have involved only certain members of the community at Skara Brae. Third, people at Skara Brae would have had an awareness of places that none of them had ever visited or been in contact with.

While there is no specific evidence to show contact between Skara Brae and other villages in Orkney, this must have taken place. The exchange of marriage partners between settlements would have been essential for the long-term health of the communities. Many villages must have contributed to the building of the major religious centres at Brodgar and Stenness and the structures now being excavated at Ness of Brodgar.

Above: An artist's impression shows villagers aboard a small boat, made from animal hide stretched over a wooden or bone frame. We cannot be sure how widely the residents of Skara Brae travelled, but Neolithic Orkney had contacts well beyond its shores.

Finally, there are certain raw materials that can only be found at specific places, like haematite from Hoy or the hard volcanic rocks found in narrow dykes across the Orkney Mainland. People from Skara Brae could have collected these materials at the source, but it seems more likely that they were acquired by barter with communities near where they were found.

Contact with communities elsewhere in Britain and Ireland is difficult to demonstrate with any certainty. Orkney was probably in contact with communities living on the Bend of the Boyne River in eastern Ireland (see pages 54–5). People were building large passage tombs there similar to Maeshowe or Quoyness on Orkney.

In Ireland, these tombs used decorated stones in their construction. At Skara Brae there are several pieces of pottery with spiral decoration, a common motif in Ireland. One fragment in particular appears to combine spirals and triangles in the same way as some stones are decorated in Ireland (see pages 54–5). This is just one piece in the evidence for links with Ireland but it suggests that some of the inhabitants of Skara Brae were involved in these contacts.

Finally, there are those items that must have signalled the existence of places beyond contact. These came adrift washed up on the western shores of Orkney. Two substances would have been particularly important. Pumice, eroded from deposits laid down by volcanic eruptions in Iceland, floated on the currents to arrive in Orkney. It provided the inhabitants of Orkney with a welcome source of abrasives for tool-making.

Equally important was wood from North America. The large rivers of its eastern coast flowed through dense, sparsely populated forests. As they did so, eroded trees were carried down to join the Atlantic currents that would in due course deposit them on Orkney's shores. Essential though these materials were to the life of the settlement, their importance in creating a sense of a wider world should not be underestimated.

Above right: A piece of haematite found at the site. The nearest source is the neighbouring island of Hoy.

DECLINE AND ABANDONMENT

No one knows why the village was abandoned. It has long been thought that a major storm, similar to that which revealed the site in the 19th century, filled the houses with sand, forcing their abandonment. However, the evidence for this is very poor.

It was Gordon Childe – the archaeologist who led the excavations of the 1920s – who suggested that a major storm was behind the abandonment of the village. His discoveries in House 7 were particularly influential in bringing him to this conclusion. He found beads in the doorway laid out in a line as though they had fallen from a broken necklace. From this, and the sand deposits he found on the floor of the house, he conjured up an evocative image of a woman breaking her prize necklace as she rushes to escape the sand filling the house. It's a wonderful story, but there is not much evidence to support it.

The position of the beads was never recorded so we don't know just how convincing the idea of a broken necklace really is. Nor was the sand deposit, supposedly brought in by the storm, much more than 50cm deep. With house walls standing several metres high it appears improbable that just half a metre of sand would cause the inhabitants to abandon the houses rather than dig out the sand after the storm was over. It seems much more likely that this sand came in with a collapsing roof and tells us nothing about the reason why the occupants left.

Our views about how and why the settlement ended come wrapped in uncertainty. What we do know is that the inhabitants did not flee in the face of an attack. There was no evidence of damage to the houses, which would be expected after a raid that led to abandonment of the village. On the present evidence it's impossible to decide whether the village was abandoned at a single moment, or whether it declined over a generation or more.

If everybody left together, the likely cause probably centred on events that rendered Skara Brae a bad place to live. Presumably, the circumstances would have had to be sufficiently serious that their own rituals could not undo the damage done. One obvious candidate is a new and infectious disease affecting either the people themselves or their animals. If there really was a great storm, perhaps the inundation of the pastures with sand was much more significant than any sand that got into the houses. Whatever it was, it must have posed an unanswerable challenge to continued survival.

On the other hand, the settlement could have been slowly abandoned as the younger members of the community declined to live in such a close-knit village. Perhaps the way of life was so constrained by established practices that there was no room for innovation. As the younger members moved away the village became increasingly households of older people. As they died houses became abandoned. The roofs collapsed and the houses became filled with sand and refuse. Eventually, they became a place for squatters such as the group that occupied a half-filled House 7 for a short period. They built a hearth in the fill, on which they appear to have cooked deer. Perhaps the abandoned house became a hunting shelter, used only occasionally.

Opposite: Parts of Orkney's coastline are now sparsely populated, but at the time when Skara Brae was occupied there may have been many more settlements.

Above: Evidence shows that deer was cooked at Skara Brae long after the houses were abandoned. The newcomers do not seem to have stayed for long.

UNDERSTANDING SKARA BRAE

This page: Professor Gordon Childe in the doorway of House 4 during the excavations of the 1920s.

Although many of our questions about Skara Brae may never be answered, we have learned a great deal since the settlement was first discovered. Our understanding has expanded partly through direct investigation of the site, but also thanks to the discovery of many other Neolithic sites in the Orkney Isles.

The existence of Skara Brae has been known since 1850. But for a long time after that we knew of no other site like it. The next site, Rinyo on Rousay, was not found until the late 1930s. But in recent years many new sites have been found. Their discovery is transforming what we know about the early farming communities in Orkney. Indeed, we now know that in the first half of the third millennium BC, Orkney was one of the most important places in Britain.

THE DISCOVERY OF SKARA BRAE

Skara Brae was first exposed by a great storm in 1850. It blew away some of the sand covering the site and exposed some of the houses, probably what we now know as Houses 1 and 3.

The local landowner at the time was William Watt, who lived at Skaill House, close to the site. He explored the two exposed houses and collected many objects. In 1861, James Farrer, who had discovered the chamber and runes at Maeshowe, undertook further work. Like Watt, he left little account of his work.

It was not until the work carried out in the 1860s that accounts of the site were published in archaeological journals. This was largely due to the frequent visits to the site of George Petrie, an able Orcadian antiquary. From his publication, and that of William Traill, we know that Watt had cleared Houses 1, 3, 4 and 5 by the end of 1867.

Above: A watercolour sketch of the site soon after it was first exposed in 1850.

The site was left undisturbed until the summer of 1913, when W. Balfour Stewart was staying at Skaill House. Among his guests was Professor William Boyd Dawkins, a geologist and archaeologist interested in the antiquity of Man and noted for his investigations in caves. They seem to have dug into House 2, but their publication is so sketchy that it is difficult to be sure of what they did.

In 1924, W.G.T. Watt's trustees placed the site into the guardianship of His Majesty's Commissioners of Works. This was the first step towards making Skara Brae the World Heritage Site it is today.

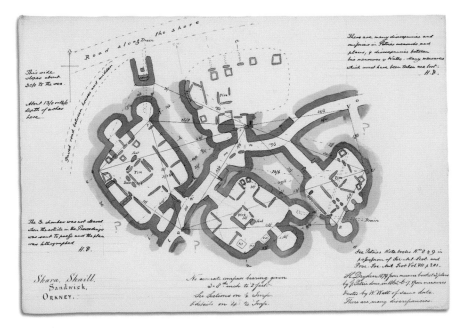

Above left: House 1 photographed in 1924, shortly before the site was taken into State care.

Above: Skaill House, residence of William Watt, the local laird credited with discovering Skara Brae. This remarkable mansion is open to visitors during the summer months.

Left: A plan of the site as excavated by George Petrie in the 1860s. At this stage, only Houses 1, 3, 4 and 5 had been cleared.

FURTHER INVESTIGATIONS AT THE SITE

With Skara Brae in State care, steps were soon taken both to protect it and to investigate it in more detail. However, this was not to be a task without complications.

In December 1924, a few months after Skara Brae had come into the care of the State, another major storm hit the site. Much damage was done to House 3. To stop this happening again, the Office of Works built a sea wall that was completed in 1926.

In 1927, a team of workmen from the Kirkwall contractor, J. Firth, began to clear out the houses under the supervision of the architect J. Wilson Patterson. In that year House 2 was fully exposed, but in the process it became clear that further work would involve removing archaeological deposits.

The responsibility for recording these deposits was given to Gordon Childe, the newly appointed Abercromby Professor of Prehistoric Archaeology at the University of Edinburgh. The emphasis, however, remained firmly on clearing the structures, as demonstrated by the fact that digging stopped once the structures ran out. Childe was left to rescue what information he could.

As a result of this approach many uncertainties remained. So further excavations were made in 1972–3 with the intention of recovering data bearing on three main questions: the date of the site; the nature of the environment at that time; and the economic basis of the village. The principal trench was between the main passage and House 7, while a smaller trench was dug near the gate, where visitors now enter the site.

Left from top: Gordon Childe and his team at the site in the 1920s; Childe greets visitors to the site; excavations underway in the 1970s.

GORDON CHILDE AND SKARA BRAE

V. Gordon Childe was an Australian who became the first Abercromby Professor of Prehistoric Archaeology at the University of Edinburgh in 1927. He was already a distinguished academic and he has become one of the most important figures in the history of archaeology. But his experience of excavation was very limited and largely confined to deep stratified sites in central and eastern Europe.

His involvement with Skara Brae began within a year of his arrival in Scotland. He had had very little time to acquaint himself with the details of Scottish archaeology but, although he could not know it at the time, Skara Brae was not going to be like anything previously found in Scotland.

More important, though, was the fact that Childe was never allowed to treat Skara Brae as a normal archaeological site. The focus of the work was always on clearing the structures so that they could be displayed to visitors. Childe was never allowed to remove structural remains in order to clarify archaeological questions. He only saw the earliest levels on the site in 12 test pits, which he was allowed to dig because there was an unrealised proposal to put a roof over the site.

These restrictions were unfortunately not the only difficulties that he had with the site. Childe was an avowed Marxist. Equally difficult for some was the flexibility he showed in his interpretations and his willingness to take on new ideas. All of this posed real problems for the conservative Scottish archaeological establishment.

The main controversy centred on the date of Skara Brae. The debate was not restricted to archaeological journals, but spilled out into the national newspapers of the day. J. Graham Callander, the Director of the National Museum of Antiquities, believed (with many others) that Skara Brae dated to the second half of the first millennium AD.

Childe seems at first to have tried to minimise the differences. His book about Skara Brae was subtitled 'A Pictish Village in Orkney', but he seemed unable to convince himself of its truth. Other writings at the same time show him changing his position. Callander never changed his view.

Above right: Childe in Structure 8 at Skara Brae.

NEOLITHIC ORKNEY

For almost a century after its discovery, Skara Brae remained unique. But in the last three decades many more Neolithic village sites have been recognised and a number excavated. These discoveries have transformed our view of Neolithic Orkney.

Not until the late 1930s was Orkney's second Neolithic village found, at Braes of Rinyo on Rousay. Limited excavation here, both before and after the Second World War, suggested that this settlement and its houses were very similar to Skara Brae.

It now looks as though there might have been many villages scattered across Orkney, although there is no reason to believe that they were all the same size. Some seem to have contained a building much larger than the houses. This may have been used for communal gatherings involving social or religious activities, and perhaps both. Whether all villages had such buildings is unclear, but we now have enough evidence to know that the layout and construction varied from place to place. Nowhere else, for instance, do we find roofed passages linking the houses, as at Skara Brae. Some of these villages may have been occupied before Skara Brae.

Above: The Stones of Stenness, about seven miles from Skara Brae, are one of the oldest monuments in the Orkney World Heritage Site.

Some, but by no means all, of the inhabitants of these villages were buried collectively in large passage tombs with a form similar to the one at Maeshowe. The tomb itself is contained within a large mound or cairn. It is entered by a long passage that leads to a central area with cells off from the sides. At the tomb at Quoyness on Sanday, carved-stone objects and a bone pin similar to those at Skara Brae were found.

People from villages like Skara Brae built the large ceremonial and ritual centres at Brodgar and Stenness. It is unclear whether they actually undertook the work, or whether they were able to use a full-time construction gang. The area has long been known as the site of the only two stone circles in Orkney, but recent work at the Ness of Brodgar, the large whaleback ridge between the two stone circles, is showing that it was filled with an area of large and elaborate stone buildings.

The largest of these buildings is more than 20 metres long and almost 20 metres wide, with walls five metres thick. These large buildings appear to have had stone tile roofs. Internally they were decorated with a good deal of art, some of which was painted. Further recent work at Ring of Brodgar has suggested that the stones are composed of different sandstones drawn from various locations across Orkney. This pattern of Orkney-wide contributions may be mirrored in the large buildings at the Ness that were perhaps erected by different groups from across the archipelago. This group of buildings was separated from the stone circles by massive walls.

Much of this was taking place at the same time as other groups across Orkney, using a different type of pottery, were living in a different style of house (like that at Knap of Howar, Papa Westray) and burying some of their dead in different forms of chambered cairn. We are still uncertain of the relationship between these two groups.

Above: The Ring of Brodgar, another important element of Orkney's Neolithic ceremonial landscape.

Below: Two carved-stone objects and a bone pin, included as grave goods in a burial at Quoyness on the Orcadian island of Sanday. The resemblance to objects found at Skara Brae is striking.

BEYOND NEOLITHIC ORKNEY

We do not know what prompted these remarkable developments among the early farming communities of Orkney. It does not seem to have involved people coming from outside the islands. Its effect, though, was to make Orkney a very important place in Britain and Ireland, and perhaps even beyond.

Archaeologists call the pottery used by the inhabitants of Skara Brae and the other villages Grooved Ware. Making pots in this tradition appears to have begun in Orkney. It is the single most common indicator of the extensive contacts that the elite in Orkney had with the rest of Britain and Ireland. Mainland Scotland, Ireland, especially the Boyne Valley, and southern England were particularly important points in the established networks. We can see these contacts expressed in a number of ways.

The southward spread of Grooved Ware seems to have been accompanied by the use of timber and stone circles, and ditched enclosures known as henges. The use of tall, thin stones to make stone circles in western Scotland seems to be closely linked with Grooved Ware, which is otherwise not at all common in the west of Scotland.

Below: A kerbstone found at the monumental Neolithic tomb at Newgrange in the Boyne Valley of Ireland. It is carved with lozenges and spiral motifs.

Connections with the Boyne Valley in eastern Ireland seem to have been particularly close. The style and form of the passage tombs built by Grooved Ware users in Orkney to bury some of their dead were adapted from those of the Boyne, both sharing a particular interest in marking through them an interest in the midwinter solstice.

Other shared elements include the use of some types of macehead and the adoption of spiral decoration, found on pottery fragments from Skara Brae. The motif also occurs on carved-stone balls found in mainland Scotland, a further indicator of contacts with that area. A pointer to even more distant contacts down the Atlantic coasts is the appearance of the Orkney vole, which is not found elsewhere in the British Isles, and may have come from France or Spain.

There may have been direct contacts between Orkney and Wessex in southern England. Excavations at Durrington Walls, a major site near to Stonehenge, have recovered pottery suggesting such connections. They have also produced suggestions of similarities in house design, even though the Durrington houses are constructed entirely of wood.

Neolithic Orkney seems to have participated in a widespread network linking the most powerful and important regions. So it is notable that very little trace has been found of the bronze weapons and ornaments that began arriving in Britain around 2500 BC. It seems that the Orkney elites failed to recognise the importance of this new material, and that this critically damaged their standing in the networks of which they had previously been an integral part.

Above: A fragment of Grooved Ware pottery found at Skara Brae.

Right: A decorated slab found at Pierowall on the Orcadian island of Westray. In both cases, the style of decoration is similar to that found at Newgrange.

Skara Brae is one of 36 Historic Scotland sites on the Orkney Isles. A selection of the others is shown below.

BISHOP'S AND EARL'S PALACE, KIRKWALL

The 12th-century bishop's palace and the Renaissance addtions of Earl Patrick Stewart, built around 1605.

↗ At the centre of Kirkwall

🕐 Open April–October

📞 01856 871918

🚗 Approx **25 miles** from Skara Brae

BROCH OF GURNESS

Orkney's most complete Iron Age village, with a broch at its centre and an entrance causeway designed to impart a sense of arrival.

↗ At Aikerness, 14 miles NW of Kirkwall on the A966

🕐 Open April–October

📞 01856 751414

🚗 Approx **15 miles** from Skara Brae

MAESHOWE CHAMBERED CAIRN

The finest chambered tomb in western Europe, dated to about 3000 BC and aligned to the midwinter sun.

↗ 9 miles W of Kirkwall on the A965

🕐 Open all year, by guided tour only

📞 01856 761606

🚗 Approx **10 miles** from Skara Brae

BROUGH OF BIRSAY

This tidal island was a Pictish village and later a Viking settlement with a Romanesque church at its heart – and what may have been a sauna.

↗ At Birsay, 20 miles NW of Kirkwall off the A966

🕐 Open when tides allow, June–September

📞 01856 841815 (Skara Brae)

🚗 Approx **8 miles** from Skara Brae

For more information on all Historic Scotland sites, please visit our website
To order a wide range of gifts, visit **https://shop.historic-scotland.gov.uk**

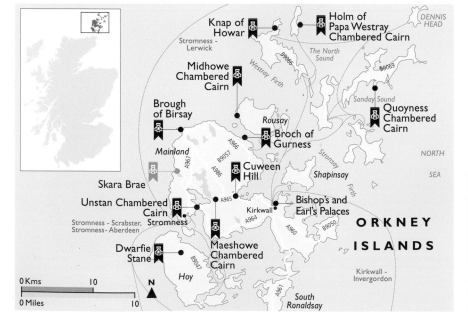

Key to facilities

Car parking	🅿
Bus/coach parking	🅿
Guided tours	
Closed for lunch	🕐
Toilets	🚻
Interpretive display	
Shop	
Strong footwear recommended	
Accessible by public transport	